Nostos

Nostos

Poems by

Anastasia Vassos

Cover design by Shay Culligan
Cover Art: Tree with Pigeon Tinos ©Gary Koeppel 2022
www.garykoeppel.com
Author Photo by Gary Koeppel

ISBN: 978-1-63980-257-9

Kelsay Books
502 South 1040 East, A-119
American Fork, Utah 84003
Kelsaybooks.com

For Donna
For Gary

In memory of my parents Jerry & Katherine Vassos

Acknowledgments

My thanks to the editors of the following journals where some of these poems first appeared, sometimes in alternate versions:

Ibbetson Street: "To Make Suffering Go Away"
Lily Poetry Review: "Viewing Actaeon & Artemis on a Greek Vase After Leaving Him at the Station"
Mason Street Review: "Translation"
Nixes Mate: "Etymology" (p. 28), "Waiting for the Barbarians," "The Barrow"
One Art: "Nostos" published as "Late Afternoon"
Passager: "Dear God,"—awarded honorable mention in *Passager*'s 2022 Poetry Contest
Poetry in the Bar Podcast: "To the Sea"
Rust + Moth: "The Lesser-Known Riddle of the Sphinx"
Voices Amidst the Virus anthology (*Lily Poetry Review*): "Waiting for the Barbarians"
Willows Wept Review: "In Kavala"

My gratitude to Kelsay Books for believing in these poems and ushering this book into the world.

Thank you dear poetry cohorts Sandy Chadis and Kyle Potvin: your careful reading of the manuscript made it better.

Thank you to the writers at Concord Poetry Center where some of these poems were birthed. You know who you are.

Thank you to Two Sylvias Press and Headlight Review for honoring this manuscript, in slightly different form, as a finalist for their chapbook contests.

A shout out to Kelli Russell Agodon for believing in my words. And just because.

Contents

Contents

For the time being
the journey forward
reckons the return home.

Viewing Actaeon & Artemis on a Greek Vase
After Leaving Him at the Station

What did you think
would happen.
How did you think
it would end.

When you took his hand.
When you traced his palm.
On the platform
near the tracks
when you saw him
through smoky glass.

It was the rough
of a sheepskin vest
the scent of cologne.
The torn remnant of his voice.
That made you want to stay.

What lonesome question.
What awful turning
around the bend
beyond the curve.

Achilles in the Twentieth Century

I was boneless at birth.
I slid along the veined alleys

of my mother to enter. My father
in the waiting room, smoking.

It was the middle day
of the middle month. Middle

of the century. Now I stand alone
on the beach, in a field. Dry grass at my feet.

My friend is sick. My friend is dying.
Who am I to complain of loneliness.

The shaded region of my fear
is the shadow clutching my heel.

Almost Father's Day

I was born the day before
Father's Day a slightly different gift
for a man who had been to war and stepped
over corpses on the beach at Normandy
and wanted a baby girl more than anything
because of the little girl in the French countryside
he gave up a hard-boiled egg to
when she had nothing to eat
one of only two stories about the war
the other one about the guy
in the foxhole who wanted
to desert and Daddy asked him
what will your mother think of you
my mother told me the story
how she forged my signature on a card
that first Father's Day *Love, Ann*
the day after I was born
I was only hours old
a gesture cute in a cozy pony kind of way
she did it because she loved
my father and knew what a daughter
meant to him because of that little girl in France
we became a family that day
he lived to almost 100.

The Poet Compares Her Father to Basho

I sit here
in the lamp's
skirt of light—
tell me, Basho
how to make poems
what to make
of adjective and noun
subject, verb.

Each poem is the only poem
and each moment
the only moment
we step into and step into…

My father used to say
the best part
of the journey
was coming home.

The journey itself is home.
There, you see
you are not much different
from my father.

He walked, too
covered miles to his store
near the Great Lakes
near the Baptist Church.

Each step is the first step—
My head bends over
the precarious page
as I write this.

Etymology

Grit of the Greeks
rubs into the cave
my mother bit words
into my cheek.

*

She dropped pepper
on my mouth once—I said
shut up I was only ten
and what did I know
—to teach me.

*

The sparrow has returned
to the nest again
this spring the chicks
utter faint,
shrill bully jays hover.

*

After I learned Greek
I applied an origin of word
scatology—the study of—
my mother no longer
around to bite my lips.

*

My tongue confined
to translating
what's been spent
saying prayers
to the so-called dead.

*

And the woodpecker far away.

Translation

Standing on the spine
of the Berkshires   I look
toward the Midwest
holding reins   arrest
wild horses   drub
the chest   I look to where
I was born   tongues
borne into evangels   smoke lifts
in the hills   mist
over a lone great lake   I shade my eyes
with the palm of my hand
I hear my body parts   speak their own
backbone erect   consequence
reaction   I was a girl   I opened
a forbidden jar and what flew out
femur   cerebrum   teeth
every word   I can think of   a stepping stone.

Ordinary Days

the clothes on the line
have bodies inside them
flown in by wind
the sun's thick scorch
diffuses afternoon
earth and soar
my mother scolded me
for flying a kite with Rob Myers
when I was 21 the age
of enlightenment childish
thing to do in the middle
so she said
of a field beside Lake Erie
my clothes feel shredded
like antique linen
as if my bone stretch moves
so far past the tight sizes
of my ordinary days
what is it about flying a kite
that lassoes my attention
beside bodies of water
it's the thing children do
hold time at the end
of a retied rope tug it
willing it to fly up
above the temporary earth
tail swagging
in the wind colors
translucent against sun's lariat
the one time
I was happy that year Rob
beside me smiling

The Land Mass of Greece Is Water

Rain today, and my smoke tree clouds
the yard with bloomclusters

frothing red against the sky. I am made
of water and salt.

Boston during a cold summer spell.
I miss the sunny three-fingered peninsula

that reaches into the Aegean east of Thessaloniki.
The first two fingers on my right hand

purse my thumb to make the Orthodox sign
of the cross across my body. I am wholly

descendent to Sappho, Homer, the Red Sox
Plato. Hot flashes rumble my blood

muscle and thunderstorm
brewing. On her last visit to Greece

my mother and her two sisters
left a note in the elbow of an almond tree.

My sister and I never argued
but for this: what temperature

to keep the thermostat
while our mother was dying.

My Aegean

Mnemonic of my beginnings
you stand between me and ancestors.
I step into your vowels to remember.

Keeper of secrets that ride your back,
you clean my grief.

In Thessaloniki I walk your waterfront—
      a dead cat floats
in your heft.

Goddess, what did I lose
in your depths.
What will I forget.

In Kavala

fresh peaches
eaten on the beach
more juice than pulp
orange and yellow
my chin
the air
eggplant tomato sandwiches
the Aegean
mussels we peeled
off the bold
sunbathing rock
knifing them open
squeezing lemon
while salt tightened
our skin
my gold baptismal cross
lost at the boulder's base
then found then lost
a second time

To the Sea

Greek men display their love for one another
by placing their arms around
each other's shoulders
lifting their knees
their trousers expose skinny ankles
flowing their brother-river
counter-clockwise dancing their *tsamiko*
across worn boards
in a taverna on the hem
of Thessaloniki
tracing spheres with their feet
bouzouki and clarinet blare
what began millennia ago.
The sea remembers them.
Their arms are so old
faces gray with stubble of beard
sweat beaded in the furrows
of their leathered skin
fingers nicotined and stained
with the work of living
their mouths contorted
in ancient concentration
their movements the maneuvers of snakes
suspended in grass waiting
then slithering the grease
beneath their soles slick with history
and who has swept the floor before them?
So, they dance, become young
suddenly arousing the clock hands
backwards to another time
when they were covered with moss
the salt of the sea
the smell of women in their nostrils.

Tomorrow they will while away
time in the *kafenion*
play backgammon
smoke cigarettes
complain about arthritis
forget the old days
when their arms stroked the sea
stroked back, up, over, strong—
and brought the Aegean to their chest.

Phosphenes

Your headstone is missing
we were going to go
with the same
font as Father's stone
my sister and I like it
but you did not
Garamond italic you thought
was not readable
not bold enough
we toss it back and forth
hesitate and already
it has been an eternity.

    *

I am studying the trees
to learn
to live without you
I am climbing the closest one
everything is closed
almost everything
the eyes of the world are shut
if I press my hands to my lids
stars, galaxies vent past
as if there is no ending
as surely there must be
I wonder
if you can hear me
if there is life
after we leave this.

Odysseus in Hades

We dress her in that smart brocade
suit her sister gave her.
The filigree buttons' graven tracery
tells yesterday's story.

The priest roils oil and dirt
in the form of a cross
on the suit. *Wash me with hyssop
and I shall be pure,*

*cleanse me and I shall be whiter
than snow.* He turns, he swings
the censer. They close the lid.
Incense carries our cries

upward toward heaven,
if there is one.
                    In my garden
black-eyed Susans elbow
their way up from down below

the earth, staking claim.
The cemetery a mile
from home. I'll pick the Susans
tomorrow, take them to her,

step on her grave gingerly,
so we both occupy the same rectangle
of ground. Unlike Odysseus in Hades,
who reached for his mother three times

and embraced nothing but shadow,
I'll drop my arms to my sides, tell her
she looked just as beautiful
as when she was alive.

The Lesser-Known Riddle of the Sphinx

There are two sisters: one gives birth
to the other—she, in turn, gives birth

to the first. Who are the sisters?
Call me the three-legged sister.

In a pride of lions, the hunters are female.
They kill their prey by strangulation.

Sphinx: from the Greek, for *squeeze*
for *anything that binds tight.*

Sphinx: head of a woman, immense—
body of a lion, wings of a bird.

We were small. We chased each other
around the yard, day and night.

Etymology

A painter tells me that the argenteum in Pissarro's rendering of leaves doesn't exist in nature.

The leaves' undersides
fluoresce as I cycle past.
The air is full of sentiment.

I see that silvergreen curling
everywhere. No one sees me
down this road.

Cycle—from Latin *cyclus*
from Greek *kyklos*—
circle of time
when phenomena
echo back to us—

Morning's silence whistles
into me. Carbon, steel circulate
under bone and muscle.

Last night I promised to pray
for a stranger's husband.

What do I know
about speaking to God.
I wear a mask.
What do I know.

Dear God,

I saw you today in the grocery store
stacking pomegranates. I recognized your dreadlocks.

I saw you holding my American Heritage dictionary
page 48 searching all the words with Greek roots.

There you were in the maple tree's phalanges
the blaring canopy grounded

wet leaves and the grass
stunted by November's cheek.

At 4 am you appeared behind my eyelids
in the shape of a boat—was that on purpose?—

—struts and joints and ribs
and stretchers almost shining.

Thank you for my body. Thank you for listening
to my babbling until an hour before dark.

In the park, the Orthodox priest passes
floating on his cloud of faith

his black cassock, his cylindrical hat
long and tall. I wipe dust off my shoe.

I thought that was you in soot on my finger
after I passed it through the candle flame.

Dear God,

when you see me eating in church
it's because I hunger.

Waiting for the Barbarians

Panic on the shelves.
On the other side, sickness pants
like an animal. We can't sleep.

The moon rides the hem
of waves heaving the shore.
My knees buckle into sand.

Fox in the coop leaves
hens covered in Jesus's blood.
We refuse communion.

Hand to hand, conjoined twins
must let go. I have time
to decipher the gospels.

You place my face in your hands
and I recall it now: *violence*
and *haste*—same word in Greek—

when I say *violence,* I mean
stand back. It's not safe.

Outside the Wind Howls Like a Crazy Wolf, and Mary Oliver Is Dead

In heaven dead poets congregate,
while here on earth, Boston faces
two degrees. Wind freezes
everyone's tears.

When they were alive, the air shook:
Mary. Lucie. Tony, Tony, Tony.
Outside my window salt trucks cough
up and down the street.

I'm concerned there's less time than ever,
convinced there's more poetry everywhere.
I read by the lone lamp's skirt,
drink a gallon of tea at midnight.

Snow comes down in sheets, frozen
nightgowns exhaling. The wind howls
like a crazy wolf.

In Order to See, I Place My Hand over My Eyes and Peek through My Outstretched Fingers

The sun rose this morning as it usually does
      all "tah dah" and brilliant and big-deal
            ready to make this side of the world happy

while everyone on our fragile surface crawls
      around wearing masks, washing hands
            and begging for scraps of kindness.

Kindness. Too bad it's only temporary.
      Quarantine: from the Latin for forty.
            We demand a return to normalcy

as if we'll be able—in, oh, forty days or so—
      to hand the supermarket cashier a twenty
            and get back the change we want

without fear of whatever it is we fear.
      In the meantime, masks. Latex gloves discarded
            in city parking lots and nowhere to walk

without stepping on a goddam virus.
      We are living our lives in the pocket
            of an old overcoat. When I was small

I stepped on a crack to break my mother's back. What did I know.
      I'm glad she's no longer here. She'd resist the mask
            and gloves. That's how honest she was.

To Make Suffering Go Away

His widow dresses in his clothes
to do laundry.

Two arms, a sleeve
maybe towels coughing on a line

the clap of clean clothes
vibrato of wind through warp and weft.

What's left out
dries under hot scorch.

A dog's bark percusses.
Night and dew descend.

She's huge as a moon
that refuses to set—

a tough shadow with her dukes up—
a shirt's frayed cuffs.

And she keeps taking photographs
of sunsets on the beach.

The last standing figure
in a stand of figures.

He told her once that every rose has forty petals
—this morning she counted only thirty.

Once, Everyone I Knew Was Alive

Before us
the stand of trees
the trunks mightily
the branches
have not yet leaved
and you say *look*
at the elephants
the way the tree bark
simulates their skin
like we saw in Kenya—
what could be better
than that, those giants
turning their huge trunked heads
when they heard our jeep—

I think that's where heaven
might be.

What solace, then
a tree that offers itself
to the sun slicing
shadows scissoring
across the foreground
catching the trees' impasto'ed skin
it almost ripples in the light
the way the river
the way
those elephants—
if you squint
you can see them there
in the distance
near the horizon.

The Barrow

John 12:24: …*unless a grain of wheat falls to the ground and dies, it remains just a grain of wheat; but if it dies, it produces much fruit.*

The earth is settling.
It's been over a year
and still no headstone
to interrupt
the earth's icy crust.
The guise of the sun
hits the heap
of dust.

I haven't eaten
and I hunger.
Before she died
she craved oysters
baked in rock salt.
The succulent tongues
sheltered, mute. The shells stacked
on a cracked blue plate.

The antique Greeks tied
adjective to noun—
small coin—to name *kolyva*
the mournful food they bartered
to keep alive their dead.
Odd treat that mixes
bitter and sweet.

I can see the recipe
in Mother's hand:
Boiled wheat berries.
Parsley. Yellow raisins.
Sesame seeds.

Amass the kolyva
in the shape of a burial mound
on a platter.
Sesame seeds on top
keep the final coat
of sugar from melting
into the mound.

Some recipes call
for pomegranate seeds
when they're in season.
I add six just in case.

Nostos

Birds circle:
rich entertainment
and in the middle of it
nature not quite dead.
The sun's blade makes
one last stab
across my back.

I am leaving you,
October of my grieving—
your gray head
your orange skirt flouncing
round your ankles.
I drive east in low gear
along the unmuscled arm of Ohio
heading toward November.

And as the sun falls behind me
trees huddle to mask
disaster. Darkness, unwelcome
takes over the sky.
I thank the stars for making
a colander of night.

I look up and ahead
through heaven's perforation.
The landscape shrivels past—
I am Orpheus in a dress
and Eurydice blind.
I drive under an overpass.
Lights strain, headlights on the bridge
gleam like the eye
in the head of an oracle.

Notes

"The Poet Compares Her Father to Basho"—italicized lines are Basho's, translated by Sam Hamill.

"Waiting for the Barbarians"—The title is taken from Constantine Cavafy's poem with the same title. Lines 14–15 are a variation of lines from A.E. Stallings' poem "Lost and Found."

"To Make Suffering Go Away" is for Bob & Deb.

About the Author

Anastasia Vassos was born in Cleveland, Ohio. She is the author of *Nike Adjusting Her Sandal* (Nixes Mate Press, 2021). She earned her BA from Kalamazoo College and her MBA from the School of Management at Simmons University. She is an alumna of the Colrain Manuscript Conference and Breadloaf Writers Conference. A reader for *Lily Poetry Review,* she speaks three languages and is a long-distance cyclist. She lives in Boston with her husband.

www.ingramcontent.com/pod-product-compliance
Lightning Source LLC
Chambersburg PA
CBHW051434090426
42737CB00014B/2977